Anonymus

Pretty pictures for tiny pets

With stories and verses

Anonymus

Pretty pictures for tiny pets
With stories and verses

ISBN/EAN: 9783742833969

Manufactured in Europe, USA, Canada, Australia, Japa

Cover: Foto ©Thomas Meinert / pixelio.de

Manufactured and distributed by brebook publishing software
(www.brebook.com)

Anonymus

Pretty pictures for tiny pets

ONE OF OUR TINY PETS.

PRETTY PICTURES

FOR

TINY PETS.

WITH

STORIES AND VERSES.

LONDON:
S. W. PARTRIDGE & CO.,
9, PATERNOSTER ROW.

Printed by HAZELL, WATSON, & VINEY, Limited, London and Aylesbury.

CONTENTS.

Contents.

Turkey Cock, Turkey Cock, off to your roost,
  It's more than high time you should go ;
The day is just done and the evening begun—
  Oh, why should you trouble me so ?
You make me run here and you make me run there ;
I think, Turkey Cock, you're not treating me fair.

BY THE SEA.

Ho! heave ho! Tommy will row,
  And Jacky he will steer,
And I will sit on the bow, to watch
  The bright waves coming near;
Bill, if he likes, can lie on the sand
Till we come sailing back to land.

THE HARVEST MOUSE.

TIMID, gentle, tiny
  mouse,
On the stalks you
  build your house;
But, alas! poor little
  fellow!
When the wheat is ripe
  and yellow,
    Then the harvest
      reapers come,
        And down
        falls your
        house and
        home.

B

AN AUTUMN DAY.

THE cows are gladly resting
  Amid the waters cool ;
The children stand to watch them,
  As they return from school.

A warm and hazy morning,
  With scarce a breath of air,
Has driven all the cattle
  To seek a shelter there.

The streamlet murmurs softly,
  And ripples on its way,
Refreshing flowers and cattle
  All through the autumn day.

"AMID THE WATERS COOL."

THE WAITS.

THE clear moonlight shone cold and
  bright
  On roof and window-pane,
When two blithe little Christmas waits
  Came singing down the lane.
And as they sang, the church bells
  rang
  A sweet and merry chime,
That mingled with the children's song,
  And welcomed Christmas-time.

THE WAITS.

FOLLOW MY LEADER, all in a row,
Jack and Mary, Jane and Joe;
And as we go we'll sing a song,
While Annie pulls wee Bill along,
Over the green and down the lane,
Through the village and back again,
Through the field, across the stile,
And then sit down and rest awhile.

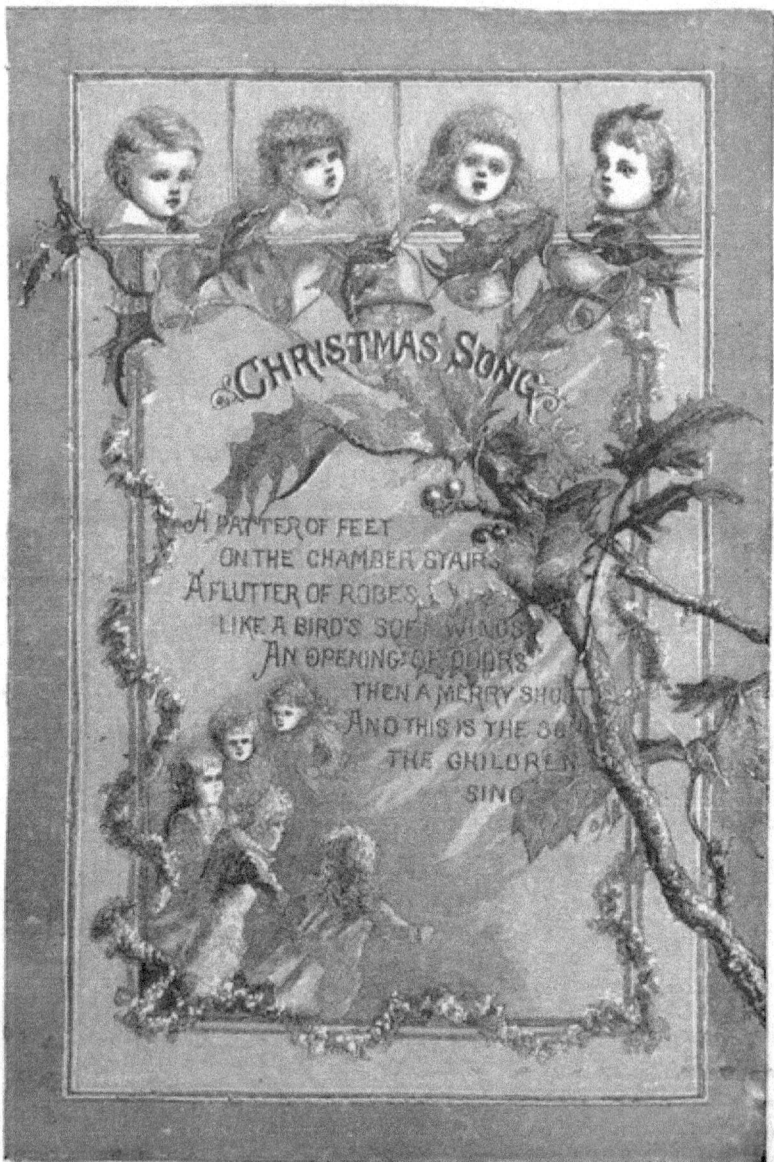

CHRISTMAS SONG

A PATTER OF FEET
ON THE CHAMBER STAIRS
A FLUTTER OF ROBES
LIKE A BIRD'S SOFT WINGS
AN OPENING OF DOORS
THEN A MERRY SHOUT
AND THIS IS THE SONG
THE CHILDREN SING

MY KITTEN.

I HAVE a little kitten,
  Just like a ball of silk;
She purrs so very softly,
  As she laps her nice new milk.

She is so full of mischief,
  So frolicsome and gay,
I've not the heart to scold her,
  Excepting just in play.

She upsets mother's workbox,
  And tangles all her thread;
She's never still one minute,
  Unless she is in bed.

POOR PUGGY.

Poor Puggy! He went out
one day
To seek a mate with whom
to play,—
He met a wasp upon the way.

"Come with me, please, my
pretty fly,
We'll wander o'er the hills so
high,"—
The wasp stung Puggy in the eye!

That night Pug to himself did say,
"One lesson I have learnt this
day:
With strangers never join in
play."

Pretty Pictures.

c

THE CHIFF-CHAFF.

THE chiff-chaff builds its nest
　　The reedy grass among;
With leaves and moss, and bits of stick,
　　It makes it soft and strong.

'Twas God who gave the bird
　　The skill to build its nest;
And taught it where to find its food—
　　The food that suits it best.

HE cares for everything,
　　E'en birds upon the wing;
And birds, and little children too,
　　Should His high praises sing.

THE CHIFF-CHAFF AND NEST.

Tom and Jack took Jane for a drive
In her car at half-past five;
At half-past six, outside the town,
The rope snapped and the car broke down.

THE AFTERNOON DRIVE.

PAYING A VISIT.

On a bough sat a bird,
  And sweetly sang
    he ;
In a stall stood a cow,
  And softly lowed
    she ;
While across the green
    grass
  A lambkin, in glee,
Skipped away, while
    the birds
  Flew over the tree.
To all these dear
    creatures
  Came Mary, to say,
" I've come with my doggie
  To wish you good-day."

WAITING FOR PAPA.

HERE are Jane and Tom and Bill
　　Upon the garden-wall,
Where the green ivy climbs and clings,
　　And gleams of sunset fall.

But why are Jane and Tom and Bill
　　Now gazing down the lane ?
They wait and watch for their papa,
　　Who went to town by train.

" Pa's coming now!" cry Tom and Bill ;
　　" Come fast, dear Pa !" cries Jane ;
And down they jump, and off they run
　　To meet him in the lane.

They bring him home, and then, for joy,
　　They clap their hands and sing—
" Dear Pa has come; let's all join hands,
　　And dance round in a ring."

WAITING FOR PAPA.

You want a scrubbing, Master Rover?
You come too late, the washing's over.

Asleep and Awake

Weary, weary doll, weary Mary Jane,
Sleep awhile and rest, wake and play again.

AT BREAKFAST.

"This basin of milk I have on my knee
Makes a nice breakfast for dolly and me;
Of course I know well she can't open
    her lips,
Not even to take in the smallest of sips,
For she's all made of wood, like a table
    or chair;
But I like to pretend she is having her
    share.
The spoon to her mouth I hold for a
    minute,
And then I myself drink up what is in it.
It makes it so much more amusing to me
My breakfast to eat in this way, do you
    see."

AT BREAKFAST.

ADA AND HER DOLLS.

ADA has four dolls, as you can see in our picture. She wants to take them out for a walk, but one of them has such a dirty face that she thinks it ought to be washed first. So she went to her mother and said, " Please, mamma, let me have the tin bowl to wash Rosa. I will not spill any of the water, and will keep it from splashing over me." Her mother kindly gave her leave, knowing she would be careful. Ada said to Rosa, " Now don't you cry; I won't let the soap get in your eyes. I know you are like some naughty girls and boys, and don't like to be washed, but it will soon be over." Rosa, however, did not behave well, and so she said, " When I take my other three dollies out, you shall not go with me." She then dressed Rosa, and put her back in her cradle. Then taking Polly from the floor, she said, " If you are good while

I dress you, you shall go for a walk with me." She also took Lucy and Topsy from

the window-sill, saying to Lucy, "You have made your hair very untidy; I must brush it." Ada then took the three good dollies out with her for a walk in the garden.

An old man sat by an apple-tree;
Weary and sad and faint was he.
Some children, who were kind and good,
Plucked the ripe apples for his food,
And brought him, from a shady pool,
A draught of water clear and cool.

ORANGES AND LEMONS.

ORANGES and lemons!   Come away and play!
Oranges and lemons!   Walk along this way!
Oranges and lemons!   Take your turn and pass!
Don't be crying, Nellie ; get up from the grass ;
Do rise quickly, Nellie ; let us have a pull :
Soon the bell will tell us it is time for school ;
Time to say our lessons, time to stop our play :
Now hold tight together, and then pull away.

AT BROADSTAIRS.

To Broadstairs, far away in Kent,
Harry, to spend the day, once went.
He took his ship down to the sand
And sailed it far away from land.
He got a rod and caught a fish,
That for his dinner made a dish.
" The day is warm and bright," said he ;
" I'll have a nice swim in the sea,
And try to catch my little ship,
And, after that, I'll have a dip."
Then in he went, but soon came out,
The waves so tumbled him about.
When dressed, he saw a boy and ass
Walking among the weeds and grass ;—
" I wish to ride, boy ; I can pay.
May I mount up ? " "Yes, sir, you may."
Into the saddle Harry got.
At once the ass began to trot ;
Then flung him off, and ran away.
So ended Harry's holiday.

Within the illustration:
- Boating
- Fishing
- Swimming
- Bathing

AT BROADSTAIRS.

THE WOODEN DOLL.

I'm but a little wooden doll,
  Have neither wit nor grace ;
Am very clumsy in my joints,
  And yet I know my place.

Most people laugh at wooden dolls,
  And wooden I may be ;
But little children love me much,
  And that's enough for me.

When I am dressed in fine long clothes,
  In fur and silk and lace,
I think myself, I'm not so bad !
  And yet I know my place.

Let people laugh—I know I'm wood ;
  Wax I can *never* be ;
But little children think *I'm grand*—
  That's quite enough for me.

THE WOODEN-DOLL MAKER.

GREEDY GRACE.

LITTLE Grace Young, though she has such a pretty name, is not at all pretty in her ways. She is very greedy. One day, when a large pitcher, containing some milk at the bottom to make puddings, was left by her mother on a washing-stool, she put her head inside to get a drink. Just look what happened! Pushing her head far in to get at the bottom, she pushed the stool as well, and fell down with her head fixed tight in the pitcher!

ON a dull day, in rainy weather,
John and his doctor met together :
The doctor said, "Your tongue's too
white,
Your pulse is also far from right ;
Get early to your bed to-night."

NAUGHTY DOLLY.

My doll is so tiresome, I can't do my work—
   She's been fretting and naughty all day.
We went for a walk—not a word would she talk,
   Though I gave her some sweets on the way.

I left her, a moment, beside a clear stream ;
   I came back—she was gone ; and I found
She had tumbled right in, got soaked to the skin,
   And, poor thing, she was very near drowned.

But the pretty red paint came off her dear nose,
   And the stream bore her ringlets away—
I wish she would sleep, for, if not, she will keep
   Me away from my work all this day.

"MY DOLL IS SO TIRESOME, I CAN'T DO MY WORK."

THE KIND BROTHER.

WHAT Nellie would do without Bob, I
    can't tell;
He is such a kind brother and loves her
    so well.
That he gives up his holidays always,
    to make
Her happy; and as she can't walk, he
    will take
Nellie out in a chair on a fine sunny
    day,
Where under the shade of the trees they
    can stay.

THE KIND BROTHER.

WHERE the trees o'erhang the stream,
Sparkling in the noontide beam,
Let us sit among the flowers,
And enjoy the sunny hours.

A SUMMER RAMBLE.

THROUGH fields and lanes, one summer day,
Harry and Mary went to stray.

As hand in hand they walked
along,
They heard the blackbird's
merry song.

From the old bridge across the
brook,
At the bright fish they had a look.

From the green vale and grassy
steep,
They heard the bleating of the sheep

They saw the thirsty cattle going
Down to the stream, and heard
them lowing.

" From the old bridge across the brook,
At the bright fish they had a look."

The mowers, in the field of hay,
Wished that they might enjoy the day.

At an old well they
    stopped to drink,
And deep down heard the bucket
    clink.

The keeper of the turnpike bar
Said, " Do not wander, dears, too far."

Then for a time, beside a pool,
They sat down in the shade so cool.

And as the sun sank
    in the west,
They went back home
    to sleep and rest.

REST FROM PLAY.

LITTLE darling Minnie May,
Are you resting from your play,
Tired of catching at the ball
As it bounces from the wall ?

Dear Minnie, those who work know
    best
How sweet it is to play or rest ;
And children best enjoy their fun
When their lesson-time is done.

In your face I think I see
A smile that seems to say to me,
You are happy, Minnie May,
At your lessons and your play.

"Minnie May,
Are you resting from your play?"

THE YOUNG SINGERS.

My sis and I went
  straying
Upon a sunny day,
Went straying and went
  playing
And singing on our
  way.

We sang of vales and mountains,
  Of blossoms, birds, and bees,
Of forests and of fountains,
  Of rivers and of seas.

The snail crept out to hear us ;
  The golden butterfly
On bright wings hovered near us,
  As we went singing by.

THE BEADLE AND THE BOYS.

THE Beadle is stout, the Beadle is tall,
And the boys are lean and the boys are small.
The Beadle is robed in scarlet and gold,
The boys have scarce clothes to keep out the cold.
" Out of the way!" cries the Beadle, gruff;
" Of your tumbling I think we've had enough.
Out of the way, for the Mayor comes here!
Policemen! see that the way is clear!"

CHILDREN AT PLAY.

TINY mites you see at play—
Who so happy as are they?
Quite a room of pretty toys,
Only for *good* girls and boys.

Little teapot, doll and ball,
Mounted rider, horse and all;
Church and cottage, bird and tree—
Who would ever *naughty* be?

If their parents, good and kind,
Toys like these, for children find,
Then the little ones should say,
"We will *good* be every day!"

CHILDREN AT PLAY.

WORKING BOYS.

" I HAVEN'T, Bill, had such a time
   I don't remember when.
I started work at eight o'clock,
   And now it's just struck ten.

" A shilling and seven coppers, Bill,
   Is not so very bad.
I see you smile.   Now, tell me, mate,
   What sort of time *you*'ve had ? "

" Just twopence, Jack.   This fine, dry
     day
   Is not much use to me ;
I like to see the streets and squares
   As muddy as can be."

"TELL ME, MATE, WHAT SORT OF TIME YOU'VE HAD."

LAZY DICK.

LITTLE Dick Docket,
　With a hand in each pocket,
Goes wandering here and there—
　　You can see by his looks
　　That he does not love books,
And in work he would rather not share.

　Ah! poor lazy Dick,
　Remember how quick
Hours by minutes are flying away!
　　And don't waste your days
　　In these sad idle ways—
School and work ought to come before
　　play!

LAZY DICK.

THE LORD MAYOR'S SHOW.

HARK to the trumpets and the drums;
Hurrah! the grand procession comes!
First a great banner, red and blue,
And then a lifeboat with its crew;
And next, in gold the heralds go,
Chief leaders of the Lord Mayor's Show.
A camel next, in silk arrayed,
And then the noble fire-brigade;
Then men in armour, side by side,
Then the Lord Mayor in pomp and pride,
And with him, sitting face to face,
The grave Recorder with the mace.
Beef-eaters next and Beadle fat,
A band and Jumbo; after that
Banners and soldiers prancing proud,
And, last, a rude and noisy crowd.

LORD MAYOR'S SHOW.

tt score="4"ran

BABY'S DINNER-PARTY.

Miss Topsy, the kitten, and Master Dog Tray,
Are dining with Bobby, the baby, to-day ;
Of course Master Robin and wife are both there,
And the cock and the hen will come in for a share.

WHEN October
days have
come,
And the bees
have ceased
to hum,
To the woods and groves
we go
Where berries on the
brambles grow;
Beech and hazel nuts we pull
Till we fill our baskets full;
Or we dig the forest ground
Where the truffle balls are found;
Or along the beach we roam
Till our mother calls us home.

THE DRAWING LESSON.

I'LL be your teacher for to-day,
So please attend to what I say—
Tommy, I'll first begin with you;
You must not paint the colley blue;
Such sheep as these were never seen;
Why, some are pink, and some are
    green!
Where, Tommy, did you ever see
A purple house, or crimson tree?—
Jane, you must press your pencil lightly,
And draw your outlines very slightly;
That cottage is not standing straight,
And where's the fifth bar of the gate?
Colour and *draw* just as you *see,*
Or artists you will never be.

THE DRAWING LESSON.

A LIVELY HAUL.

A LIVELY HAUL.

WHERE the wavelets race and run,
Flashing in the morning sun;
Where they ripple to the land
And then hurry down the sand,
See, on this bright autumn day,

Three rude little boys at play.
Jack and Bill, with laugh and shout,
Pull their playmate, Bob, about ;
Haul him up the shingly strand
Like some fish just brought to land.
On the spot where they now play,
When a few hours pass away,
Waves will toss their crests on high,
And the sea-gulls flit and fly.

LITTLE BO-PEEP.

LITTLE Bo-peep
Had a pretty pet sheep,
But one day forgot to mind it;
  So it went astray,
  Through the clover and hay,
And Bo-peep went sobbing to find it.

As she passed on her way,
She met Master Dog Tray,
Who said, "Can I help you, Miss Bo-
      peep, to-day?"
  "Oh yes, please, sir, do;
  'Twill be so kind of you!"
And away, side by side, through the
      fields, went the two;

And they found the pet sheep
On a hillock asleep—

Oh! how glad and how thankful was
Little Bo-peep.

HOW TO DRAW A PIG.

THE body of piggy
　　Is shaped like a bean,
Except when he's poor
　　And uncommonly lean.

Then give him two ears
　　And a long and strong
　　　　snout—
He'll find it so useful
　　For rooting about.

Also two little eyes ;
　　And make, without fail,
At one end a mouth,
　　At the other a tail.

Then add four short legs,
　　And you have a whole
　　　　pig
Who can run for his food,
　　Be he little or big.

THE VASE THAT BECAME AN OWL.

WHAT is this? just
    Guess and try;
You will find out
    By-and-by.

It is changing,
    You can see,
And is growing
    More like me.

Changing still,
    More like it grows;
Now you see my
    Eyes and nose.

Changing still,
    Now guess and try;
" A staring Owl!"
    Yes, that is I.

BABY'S RIDE.

Tom said to me one day, "We'll give
   Our brother Jack a ride ;
His cart shall be a railway-car,
   And he shall sit inside.

" An engine Bill and I will be,
   To pull the car about,
And you will be the guard, to see
   Jack does not tumble out."

We trotted gently up the hill,
   And home we galloped back ;
Tom, Bill, and I enjoyed the run,
   And so did brother Jack.

BABY'S RIDE.

THE SHOWMAN'S SONG

WALK up! Walk up!
And see the show.
    There's no better.   Strike up, Joe!
    Beat and bang upon the drum ;
    We must make the people come.
    Come away, my little dear.
    Walk up ! Walk up ! Please pay here !

HOW TO DRAW A ROOSTER.

WHAT is this?
  A mutton chop,
Just come from
  The butcher's shop!

Place a head
  Upon the chop,
On the head
  A comb and crop;

Place a tail
  Upon the chop.
Don't forget,
  Before you stop,

Two stout legs,
  And claws also;
Then, perhaps,
  The cock will crow.

WILD RABBITS.

Where the berries, black and ripe,
　Hang upon the brambles,
Where the grass grows thick and tall
　Master Bunny gambols.

Sometimes at his door he sits,
　When the days are sunny,
Winks his eyes and wags his ears,
　And chats with Mistress Bunny.

Play, dear rabbits, while you may,
　Crop the short, sweet grasses ;
For the winter days will come
　When October passes.

Pretty Pictures.   WILD RABBITS.

ROBIN'S BREAKFAST.

THE cold snow has come,
And poor Robin's home
Is dreary and lonesome indeed;
So good Willie Guest
Is doing his best
To give little Robin a feed.

Every morning at eight
He will go to the gate
And call little Robin to come:
While the frost and snow last
Poor Robin won't fast,
Nor be needing a seed or a crumb.

ROBIN'S BREAKFAST.

FISH AND FISHING.

THIS is the FISHER who sailed away
From the harbour bar at the close of day.

This is the BOAT, with sail and oar,
That bore him away from the sandy shore.

This is the NET that he spread around
When the boat arrived at the fishing-ground.

These are the FISH, eel, haddock, and ling,
A dainty dish for a queen or king.

This is the LIGHTHOUSE whose
gleaming ray
Guided the fisherman over the
bay.

And here's the FISHMONGER,
from whom is bought
The fish that the hardy fisherman caught.

Children dear, when the night-winds roar,
Think of the FISHERMEN far from shore,
And pray to God to guard and keep
All who are out on the stormy deep.

TITTY-TOTTY

LITTLE TITTY-TOTTY,
  Toddling up the lane,
Little Titty-Totty,
  Toddling down again ;
Eyes so full of wonder
  At the bright blue skies,
At the buds and blossoms,
  Bees and butterflies ;
Wondering at the singing
  Of the birds so sweet,
  Wondering at the daisies
  Springing at her feet—
Darling Titty-Totty,
  Year will follow year,
And you still will wonder
  While you see and hear :
Wonder at the goodness,
  Wonder at the love,
And the tender mercy,
  Of our God above.

LITTLE TITTY-TOTTY.

THE TWO TRUANTS.

EDWARD and John were idle
boys,
And fond of mischief and of
noise.
One time, from school they
stayed away,
And this is how they spent
the day—
They stoned the rabbits and
the rooks,
The frogs and fishes in the
brooks.   [brown;
They saw a squirrel white and
John said to Ned, " Let's knock it down."
The stone, however, harmless sped,
And struck a peasant girl instead,
Who with her brothers in the wood
Was gathering sticks, and nuts for food.

NEVER GRUMBLE.

BERTHA sits in her wicker
 chair,
And to herself complains,
" I can't get out to take a walk,
 Because it always rains."
Tom, turning o'er his picture-
 book,
Says to his sister Sue,
" I'm glad the rain and snow are here,
 And so, I think, are you.
" For, when they go away, the spring
Will come with sunny showers ;
Then spring will
 go, and sum·
 mer bring
The bees and
 birds and
 flowers."

Pretty Pictures.

L

STREET CRIES.

" Milk, ho ! Milk, ho !" " Echo ! latest news ! "
" Old Clo! Old Clo!" "Brush your boots and shoes!"
" Sweep, ho ! Sweep, ho !" What a dreadful din !
One here—one there—then the rest begin.
" Pippins ! Pip-pins ! Twopence for a lot ! "
" Ting-a-ring, Ting-a-ring ! Muffins piping hot ! "
" Cop-per ! Cop-per ! Save your boots and dresses!"
" Dust, ho ! Dust, ho !" " Buy my water-cresses ! "
" Onions ! Onions !" What a horrid bawling !
Now here—now there—somebody is calling.
" Chairs to mend ! Chairs to mend ! Neat, neat,
    neat ! "
Hark to pussy mewing—" Meat, meat, meat ! "
" Ima-gees ! Ima-gees ! Madam, please do buy ! "
Oh, then ! Oh, then ! comes the loudest cry,
"All a-blowing! All a-growing! Sell them in the pot!
You shall have them very cheap. The last three I
    have got ! "

STREET CRIES.

THE GLEANER.

THE gleams of autumn's setting sun
  Along the west were glowing,
When I met little Mary May.
I asked, "Where have you been to-
    day?"
"Sir, I've been gleaning far away,
  And homeward now I'm going.

"I rose just as the morning sun
  Above the hills was peeping :
The lark was singing in the sky ;
And now so very tired am I,
That when the stars come out on high,
  I shall be soundly sleeping."

"I'VE BEEN GLEANING FAR AWAY."

PUSSY'S TALK.

GOOD-MORNING, dear young ladies!
   Don't start because you see
Your little playmate, Kitty,
   Come scrambling down a tree.

I've climbed the highest branches,
   And from the topmost bough
I saw a milk-maid milking
   A pretty snow-white cow.

I thought, now down I'll scramble,
   And hasten o'er the lea;
Then, purring, ask the milk-maid
   To give a drink to me.

PUSSY'S TALK.

MINNIE'S RIDE.

In her four-wheeled coach, on a summer day,
When the leaves are green and the flowers are
    gay,
Miss Minnie goes out for a morning ride,
Up the grassy hill by the forest's side.
This morning she'll call on her " Aunty Jane,"
At the big white house in the sunny lane,
To ask if she will come to tea;
And thankful is she to her brothers three,
Who have drawn her coach with right good
    will,
Over the meadow and up the hill,
And all for the love of their sister dear.
Now, a pull, a push, and a hearty cheer
Will rattle the coach up to aunty's door,
Who will gladly welcome the happy four.

MINNIE'S RIDE.

THE READING LESSON.

BRIGHT, through the leafy apple-tree,
  The autumn sun is streaming,
And, on that book the children read,
  With golden light is gleaming.

" Dear brother, I am sure that soon
  You'll read as well as I ;
It is not very hard to do,
  If you will only try.

" D-I-C-K—what word is that ?
  Now look, and tell me quick."
" Why, sister dear, D-I-C-K
  Is my own name—it's Dick!"

"WHAT WORD IS THAT?"

THE HEDGEROW SCHOOL.

I am the mistress of the school—
   Come, do your lessons well ;
Be careful to obey each rule,
   And mind, now, how you spell.

Each take your slate, and quickly write
   The words which I shall say;
Don't look at one another's slates,
   And, mind, we're not at play.

Whate'er you do, do heartily,
   With all your might and main,
And if you find you've done it wrong,
   Just do it o'er again.

THE HEDGEROW SCHOOL.

PRETTY PUSSY.

Pussy, you look, I do declare,
  As if you would like to speak,
Sitting upright upon that chair,
  With your fur so white and sleek.

I wonder much what you would say
  If you could talk to me;
Perhaps you would ask for a game of
    play.
  But I am too busy, you see.

PRETTY PUSSY.

HOW TO DRAW A GOOSE.

THIS is an egg,
  I think you will say;
But I will change it
  In this way—

I add a head,
  Which looks absurd,
And makes it somewhat
  Like a bird.

I add a wing,
  And legs, a pair,
One of them hanging
  In the air,

And then a tail;
  And now it wanders
To seek its brother
  Goosey-Ganders.